Adrift a Fourth Wave

Adrift a Fourth Wave

Poems by

Brenda Nicholas

Cover design by Shay Culligan

Cover art by Chloe Nicholas, "Lovers"

ISBN: 978-1-63980-013-1

Kelsay Books
502 South 1040 East, A-119
American Fork, Utah 84003
Kelsaybooks.com

for Chloe, my daughter, artist & inspiration:
you are blossoming into an independent, strong willed,
and authentic woman. I'm incredibly proud of you and know
you will soar toward your own definition of success and happiness.

Acknowledgments

My sincere gratitude to editors of the following publications for providing space for various versions of these poems:

The Worcester Review: "Mountain Pose"

Sand Hills Literary Magazine: "I See This Sculpture and Think My Back is *Not* a Wall"

Unbroken: "How to Make Boxed Shells in 8 Easy Steps"

The Ekphrastic Review: "A Chat with My Daughter About a Woman and Her Vase," "Mountain Lessons," "If This Chair Could Talk"

Evening Street Review: "Leonine Maine," "For the Woman Who Eats Dirt," & "I Need Dramamine"

They Call Us Flawed Zine: "Money as Factory," & "Imprint"

Buddhist Poetry Review: "Chair Pose"

The Avocet: "Bird of Paradise Pose"

Speckled Trout Review: "Woman on Edge"

The 3 Quarter Review: "When I finally See What Nineteen Looks Like"

Adanna: "How Long Can a Butterfly Live?"

The New Mexico Review: "Reflection," "Woman, Flower, Midsummer Night," "Spring Dance"

Snapdragon: "Three Odes to a Tactile Past"

Broke Bohemian: "Postfeminist Halloween Party"

Painted Bride Quarterly: "Bratz Dolls Ask Brunette, Roxxi Bratz, to Write Response Letter to Critics Who Say the Dolls "Encourage girls to think about themselves as sexualized objects"

The Helix: "Cinderella's Night Out"

The Jet Fuel Review: "She, Artichoke"

Menacing Hedge: "Dating Story Trilogy," "Elevator Love," and "Bird Cage"

Red River Review: "Public Spectacles"

Main Channel Voices: "Swig"

The following poems were originally included my chapbook *Hari Om, Hurry Home,* Finishing Line Press, 2021

"Bridge Pose," "Cobra Pose," "Wild Thing Pose," "Revolved Triangle," "Circling Heart Pose," "Chair Pose," "Mountain Pose," "Goddess Pose," and "Lotus Pose"

Contents

1. Lost Pearls

Disney-scape	15
Cinderella's Night Out	17
Swig	18
Bird Cage	19
Magazine Instructions for Ladies	20
Leonine Mane	21
When I Finally See What Nineteen Looks Like	22
One More Minute	24
Ice Skating Lesson	25
Imprint	27
Bratz Dolls Ask Brunette, Roxxi Bratz, to Write Response Letter to Critics Who Say the Dolls "Encourage girls to think about themselves as sexualized objects"	28
She, Artichoke	30
A Rose Is a Rose Is a Relationship	32
Depression Shows Up Like a Pimple-Spotted Teen	33
Dear God:	34
Sleeping Beauty	35
Civil War	36
Into the Light	38
Broken Pieces	39
Bridge Pose	40

2. Rain After Goodbye

Dating After Divorce	43
Suburban Serengeti	44
Woman on Edge	45
How Long Can a Butterfly Live?	46
I Need Dramamine	47

A Chat with My Daughter about a Woman and
    Her Vase   48
How We Lie under an Olive Tree   49
Three Odes to a Tactile Past   50
Paper Doll   52
Dating Story Trilogy   53
Rain After Good-bye   55
How to Make Boxed Shells: 8 Easy Steps   56
Cobra Pose   57

3. Wild Thing

Wild Thing Pose   61
At Whole Foods   62
Revolved Triangle   63
Postfeminist Halloween Party   64
Circling Heart Pose   65
Reflection on R.C. Gorman's *Reflection*   66
Mountain Lessons   67
I See This Sculpture and Think My Back is *Not* a
    Bridge   68
Gracias!   69
Money as Factory   70
Chair Pose   71
Life Broken into Thirds   72
Mountain Pose   73
Goddess Pose   74
Sisterhood   75
If This Chair Could Talk   76
New Love   77
Lotus Pose   78

1.

Lost Pearls

Disney-scape

1.

We float along a neo-real river
past shore-bound plastic, smiling dolls
waving as if we are welcomed
everywhere across the world's water.
Around this bend we affect Spain,
and the girls in white ruffled shirts and skirts
dance their Spanish dance, smiling.
Around the next bend we affect Arabia
where black veiled dolls wave at us,
unblinking by our presence.
There is a sensory explosion here,
a unifying tune. Busy people
distract our vision's every angle.
We are bamboozled by the oneness
as we pass the wishing well full of coins.
This is America, after all,
looking large in a small world.
Around the park, neo-happiness
engulfs us, embodies us with liquid blue
calories and fried everything.

2.

With a *Fastpass,* we tour traditions
of the world as our tradition:
this shiny display of wishes,
this scrubbed and waxy flash of hope,
this perpetual present.
We approach Cinderella's palace
of electrical magic. My daughter's eyes,

wide with unknowing, wonder
about the bedroom of a princess:
at what sort of diamond table does she sit
to eat with her dainty gloves,
in her gown spun of butterflies?
She vibrates. She believes. When we enter
a mosaic tiled room, and our voices echo
off this hollow hallway,
my daughter's shoulders slump
as she says, "Her castle is empty, mommy."

Cinderella's Night Out

Saturday night Cinderella slides into her micro-mini
blue dress and yellow stilettos.
She meets her friends in the parking lot
of *Chick Fil~A* where they climb into
her rusty orange Jeep Wrangler to head
downtown where a man with black hair,
dressed in black, sits on a black stool
against a black wall, and stamps their pale
hands with a black T.
A bouquet of color, they enter the bar
littered with pool tables and a band
that plays cover tunes in the back.
The linoleum dance floor is empty
because no one dances at The Thorn.
Cinderella scans for an open pool table.
A group of guys dressed in baggie jeans, tee shirts,
and black hats twisted backward,
eyeball her. The tall one glides over
and Cinderella smiles.
She does not see grime-encrusted tables
or dust piled high on frames of painted
roses. She does not feel
her feet stick to spilled beer on the floor, or
know about the pill the boy will slip in her drink.
Her eyes consume only the fluorescent-washed
face of this prince who carries a pool cue
to her as if this gift might shatter
if dropped.

Swig

A bat out of Haiti, I rev my red Jetta and speed
out of the bar's parking lot. I need a bite of coffee
from the World's End Diner. There's nothing like
a salty 4 a.m. meal to stave off a sexual appetite.
Sheepish and probably hairy, Larry smiles at me,
slides his relentless hand under my skirt as I drive
past a cop parked in the thick, snowy overhang
of pine and palm trees. Laser aimed and ready
with his toucan nose, he sniffs out a glimpse of me.
The two cops hobble up to my window, mustaches glowing
in the dark mist of winter's silence.
May I see your license and registration?
they ask me, swollen with pride at their discovery
of a drunk driver. *Gunter, glieben, glauchen globen,*
I sing with the radio, dig in my purse—pray—
that I have a registration card in one of my glove boxes.
Two Larrys, two cops, two by two the world swarms around
my sunken ark. I must act sober, I tell myself. Focus.
I open the correct box, white paper stares at me
from its proper spot. Your front headlight is out, they tell me,
better replace it before the end of time.
He hands my paper back, not knowing he's letting
Brewski loose, drunk; *faire glisser electrique.*
The cold bottle of reason stings my bitter lips as I wink
at Larry, take a quick swig from his flask and drive off.

Bird Cage

The 1920s passed with her perched
on the southwest corner of her couch
in a yellow, green, blue, or red dress
layered in fringe,
faded yellow feather boa
and long strand of pearls around her neck,
her skinny legs folded like a flamingo
on the armrest of the couch.
A long cigarette wand burned in one hand,
a tumbler full of icy cocktail jiggled in the other.
She was just south of buzzed,
day after day.
Her husband-the-important-doctor
didn't want her to work,
didn't want her to paint,
play bridge or go to typing school.
When friends stopped by to see her
she'd ask them in her quiet voice
to go out and buy her some stockings.
When they asked her what color,
she'd say it didn't matter.

Magazine Instructions for Ladies

scream messages at me at checkout stands
in many public spaces: *Lean or Lonely!*
Look Polished & Poised. Blow Every Man's
Mind! Start Your Bikini Body Meltdown Diet Now!

I am reminded of Gandhi burning passes for Indians,
how paper is oppression as destructive as empires
in need of a good torching. And I march past these racks,
think of Seshadri's poem: *we are in a fabrication;*
he wisely reminds me, *maybe even in a cartoon.*

Note: "We are in a fabrication. Maybe even a cartoon" is from Vijay Sheshadri's
poem "Personal Essay," from his book *3 Sections.*

Leonine Mane

While women marched with picket signs,
an affront to picket fences
they felt they were parked behind
like some kind of kept pet,
Gloria Steinem must have watched
Farrah Fawcett over the rims of her specs
as she shook out a freshly printed newspaper
touting Farrah's hair, *A work of art,*
a symbol of women's liberation,
proclaiming her as carefree as the rolling sea
as she sprang out, letting salted waves toss her locks
to wild. The word *mythomania,*
must have crossed Gloria's lips as she read
those reporter's words. All of this fuss
over tresses, this sea lion's mane.
And the feminist movement inched on.
All the while, Farrah and her hair
climbed a ladder over the top of fame.
Charlie's Angels reached number one,
and what did Gloria think
when she read Farrah's response:
it's because none of us wear a bra.

When I Finally See What Nineteen Looks Like

1

There are certain sounds I'll never forget,
like the depressed shuffle of my mom's slippers on wood floors
and words like "I told your dad you might not be his
when you were two years old. We were driving in the car."
I was home from college, eager to see old friends,
ready for a summer job,
and I wondered why I was surrounded by bags of recyclables
on the back porch.

My mother's leg dangled over the papasan chair
and swung incessantly back and forth
as she rolled a tiny wad of paper between her fingers.
Her movements always caught the greater part
of my attention, made me think of weakness. I took out a cigarette,
and she said, "I wish you wouldn't smoke—
Give me one," and we puffed away for the same reasons.

She loved that papasan chair, I think,
Because she was cradled by it.
None of this is for me, I remember telling myself—
The papasan, the swinging leg, the uncertainty.

2

15 years later, my two-year old daughter tells me
she has the hiccups.
When did she learn that word?
This tiny, two-foot walking sponge who drinks up life
can't even write her own name, yet she laughs at jokes
and loves putting puzzles together.
My nineteen-year-old babysitter arrives,
stands in the doorway, shyly shifts her weight,
tells me she's pregnant. Her boyfriend dropped her off.
They plan to get married. She shoves her Care Bear key chain
into her pocket.

Last month she dated a different guy who, she had said,
was handsome but home-schooled, so he failed
the army's entrance exam.
Last month my babysitter was joining the army, too,
but why dwell on the past? Tonight, she's watching my kids.

My mother was nineteen when I was born,
and my father was drafted during the Vietnam War.
He was one of ten not sent. I can't help but realize,
as I notice my babysitter fidget,
that she is my mom, and the clandestine shadow
pulling out of the driveway is my dad.

One More Minute

for Chloe

Of your tiny, determined fingers on the keyboard playing
      songs of broken hearts you do not yet know,
Of the word love you write inside hearts
      you draw on my envelopes, calendars, notebooks,
Of your nightly plea for one more minute of me
      lying next to you at bedtime,
Of you in my closet, wearing my shoes, my scarves, my hats,
      my present, your future.

Ice Skating Lesson

for my father

You asked me to skate with you around the entire lake.
It was late afternoon, already near night.
I looked out past my homemade rink;
the expansive frozen lake stared back.
I felt small, far away from the farthest shore.
Beyond our smoothed rink, we hit ice warts.
Snow ghosts drifted across our path.
I tripped, feared weak ice that might exist,
could—at any moment—open to a monstrous mouth,
chew us up with ice shard teeth, push us down with the fish.
Let's go back, I said. *Not until we get around the whole lake,*
you said. *This is the beach where we drive our boat,* you pointed.
My summer memories had iced over,
covered with white snow puffs,
familiar motor hum & fish splash sounds swallowed
by wicked wind that slices skin.
My frosty feet tingled as we reached the deepest part
of the lake where the all-eyed eels lived.
You joked that the ice better not break there.
Let's go back, I said again. *Are you Kidding?* You said again.
No way! We're half-way around. We have to finish!
My tired, wobbly legs pressed on.
Darkness descended, and the magnitude of this
adventure hit me with full force.
I was Nancy Drew on the surface
of a strange undiscovered planet!
My confidence grew with each scrape
of my skates on solid ice.
My form improved. I sped up.
You let go of my hand,
and I practiced Dorothy Hamill spins.
When I saw the lights from our house appear,

my shoulders sank. *Let's go around again!* I said.
Are you kidding? Not tonight! you said.
My blades had slid across every inch
of the lake's rim, I realized then,
as we reached our tiny backyard rink.
That was the day you taught me
the distance between my yard and the scary world,
how to measure it—persistently—
one ice skate blade after the other.

Imprint

I ride my bike with my ten-year-old daughter
following me along a wooded path like a duckling.
We left our phones at home, stepped away from devices
because they dull what should be sharp,
It's America, after all, home of abundant choices.
We peddle our way to Diane Landry's museum display,
and the first piece we see is a washing machine.
Digital heads of women hover:
their blunt eyes stare, unsmiling, handicapped of joy,
jostling back and forth like fabric,
these girls and mothers from the past
dutifully wash as if washing will end.
I watch my daughter's dismayed reaction
to progress standing still in our nation.

Bratz Dolls Ask Brunette, Roxxi Bratz, to Write Response Letter to Critics Who Say the Dolls "Encourage girls to think about themselves as sexualized objects"

Dear Sirz:

We don't agree with your criticizms of us at all! Yes, we have dilated pupliz and pouty lips, but we believe our disproportionate headz signify the importance of having brainz over boobz, so it offendz us when critics say we are overly sexxualized.

We are given clothez appropriate for our favorite placez & pastimez, such az shopz, nail salonz, clubz, bandz, datez & moviez, and short dressez are the fashion! At least we wear pantiez—unlike Barbie.

We are in a modern world now. Barbie is a relic. It is long past time for dollz to represent America'z emergence into a more tolerant space. Gone are the Aryan dominated dayz wherein blondz ruled the world.

It iz true, our manufacturer uzez one mold to cast us so our bodiez and facial featurez are exactly the same. However, our hair colorz represent global diversity, and some of us are even dyed darker skin shadez.

Sure, it is more uncomfortable and embarrassing to loze a shoe, since our lower leg iz attached to it. Once, Cloe had a difficult time dancing with one shorter leg. We laugh about it now.

The bottom line iz, young girlz relate to Bratz dollz. We represent the most important idealz for young women. We represent the American dream, and when girlz play with us, they are able to practice living the livez they too can achieve if they work hard enough.

Yourz,

Bratz Dollz of America

She, Artichoke

1598

Buttoned up to the top of her neck,
Mademoiselle Roussel reaches
for the artichoke. At the supper table
her uncle slaps her hand and fork away, explains,
"Artichokes are not for the ladies!"
Now she is certain she will faint. Flushed
in her heavy dress, she falls to her knees
near her mother, who whispers that the artichoke
is an aphrodisiac, and the women bow their heads
back into their slight pieces of stale bread.

1947

Norma Jean flashes her hungry smile,
waves to the crowd lining Main Street.
Every eye in Castroville, California drinks up
her strapless blue chiffon dress,
tight around her waist and short enough
to show her shapely legs.
Her blonde hair blends into the sun, a halo
that hovers over the daisy–covered float.
The parade ends at the Kiwanis Club parking lot
where newspaper photographers swarm like gnats,
while the mayor declares her
Castroville's First Artichoke Queen.
He beams with pride and tops her head
with a handcrafted floral crown. In 1947,
the Artichoke Capital of the World feeds
Marilyn Monroe sautéed artichokes
soaked with sugar.

2012

Featured in *Food Fashion,* models
pose wearing edible outfits.
A blonde adorns a *Cream Puff*
Wedding ensemble. Rows of airy pastry
dangle from her, stacked in triangular form.
She is a statue of dessert.
She is her own wedding cake,
ready for her groom to consume her.

Another wears the *German Chocolate Bubble Dress*
designed with perfectly molded candy that clings
to the model's breasts, billows out
at her hips, suggests creamy delight
underneath her scrumptious skirt.
The model in the *Elegant Artichoke Heart Gown*
is covered with spears of artichokes.
She looks dangerous, like a porcupine,
well protected like an armadillo, or
as unattainable as a mermaid,
but the outfit exposes her soft black bra,
reveals touchable tenderness. The caption says:
"Artichokes don't always look *this* good
on a dinner plate."

A Rose Is a Rose Is a Relationship

I eat his roses for breakfast,
each petal a velvet lie
dissolving on my tongue
like communion wafers
after confession.
I must forgive myself
for believing him before today.
Each thorny stem I chew & swallow
scrapes my throat like fangs,
like claws gouging out a path
to my voice, where
leaves & vines grovel
in dirt toward roots
as if planting a seed
at my base
could possibly regrow it.

Depression Shows Up Like a Pimple-Spotted Teen

to take a nap, to take a drag—hell—
to smoke the whole pack, to point out what is *not*
or doesn't, what love *doesn't* look like:
a gulf green browned
where sun sunk his fiery teeth,
a badly bruised apple Eve bit into
and spit out like a coward,
like the runt of a rose garden at the end
of her row, next to a neighboring weed
who—daily—forces his spindly arms around her,
no matter how often she scratches him
with her thorny nails.

Dear God:

I accidentally cast my pearls
before swine. I admit
I spent my twenties
drunk on gin and love.
You provided me with pearls, God,
or you could say I inherited tiny, round,
valuable crystalline forms
from my mother. For years
I kept them buried,
safe within my iridescent womb,
and then, in my constant haze,
mistook an omnivorous ungulate
for a great pearl hunter
adorned in shiny diving gear.

Sleeping Beauty

A wave of fatigue floods my body
as if pricked in the hand by a poisonous pin.

It travels through my bloodstream
until I crawl into bed, let my mind sink back

to a younger me when my fiancé and I dined
at El Matador on sopapillas, margaritas & smothered burritos.

We'd sit under a rainbow spectacle of stuffed parrots,
sombreros, guitars & painted suns. Stale lard

clung to curtains, tablecloths, the floor, but I cared
only for the food in my mouth & the look in his eyes

before time spun spools of pain around & stuck me
alone dawn after dawn with unpaid bills, melancholy kids,

a need to slip through the cracks in my sheets,
revisit the castle, slip my thumb in the thimble

& use the needle to unstitch his lips from mine.

Civil War

History repeats
on musty 8-tracks,
hissing cassettes,
large looping film reels
spinning around,
whipping that constant click,
unfeeling, regardless
of *It's a Wonderful Life,*
or *Gone with the Wind*
brimming full of burned homes
and heroines screaming
great balls of fire!
That heavy thump
of black snake belly
we call the past
constantly rewinds,
plays, rewinds.
What is Civil about War?
My husband and I were
two countries by the end,
an invisible border
split down the center
of our bed. We shared
a history: he became
his alcoholic father.
I became a young,
misguided bride,
like my mother, stubborn
and belly full of broken
romance tapes unspooling
blind defeat. War breeds
more wars. Noble motives
defend hostilities,

but before long, spools
of fire color walls
and faces red, enflame
porches and broken-
down homes, regardless
of the fancy address.

Into the Light

He said I was impetuous
like the deer that saw the light,
heard the motor, but still darted
straight into my headlight.

As if ending my marriage took me
only a second to decide.
If I were the deer and my marriage the car,
I would stand at the road's shoulder
for five years—paralyzed by fear—
wondering whether to cross
or stand safely in bushes.

If I were impetuous, it was the day he proposed,
and I said yes. In my youthful, misguided way
I saw a light in his eyes, ran fast,
and fatally crashed into his heart.

Broken Pieces

White clouds break blue sky as earth cracks
under the weight of *Nilch'i Dine'e'*'s Second World:
adultery & scandal scatters them to four corners.
Only a shadow in the distance remains
unbroken from its woman.

Nothing lasts like my father's old stereo, anymore:
not employment, not electronics, not marriages.
Houses housing broken homes still stand
and watch as broken people pack up
their fractured families, attempt to pick up
the pieces and Frankenstein them back together.

Bridge Pose

Yoga means yoke, to connect as a bridge connects
disconnected land between spirit and body
because brain pushes pain aside like a fascist
on a propaganda-inspired deleting spree.
Meanwhile, body harbors agony: organs, muscles,
vessels become burial plots, graves trapping trauma,
grasping a ripped photo, a dropped glass.
Invisibly fragile passion evaporates into air after
final words are spoken, but body holds onto lost pieces,
even as a home you shared with a man you loved disappears
into your rearview mirror as you drive away.

2.

Rain After Goodbye

Dating After Divorce

is deep sea fishing for halibut, shark, or ship wreckage.
It is online shopping for broken bits returned to invisible
shelves floating among flotsam. Have I transformed
into an enormous salmon? These broken fishermen
don atrophied muscles, unable to pull me onto the boat,
too tired and spent from their last fishing trip.
Sometimes I feel a tug, then something feels offline.
After two platonic dates, a man's hungry voice
swallows me, tells me he "misses me."
What is to miss, already? I am scared
of fast swimming fish, pointed, ready, heading
to drag my babies and me to the Great Pacific
Garbage Patch—that plastic bag vortex
collected from around the world—where we could
wind up wound around bellies of baby sea animals.

Suburban Serengeti

On my second lap around, I notice an old woman
walking her dog, holding a leash in one hand,
golf club in the other. I glance down at my mace,
and this reminds me of a single woman
who lived in our small town when I was a girl.
She had made the news: stabbed twenty times
by a construction lion who spotted her
mowing her brush in her suburban habitat.
The news mentioned the bikini she wore
to catch some rays as she tended her yard,
but it didn't bother to mention what her killer did
after his hunt. Did he snore the afternoon away
in his den—belly full and satisfied?

Woman on Edge

After R.C. Gorman's Canyon de Chelly Twilight

The moonlight paints on her
a blood-red shawl with definitive lines
that trails her body's length.
She hovers, diminutive, at a cliff's lip.

When she whispers secrets into this black canyon,
the rocky cheeks blush,
and the stars sharpen like fangs
in the open blue mouth above,
ready to swallow.

How Long Can a Butterfly Live?

In 1976 a photographer catches Farrah,
casts her in a net. She sits
with her left arm on bent knee,
mounds of blonde pile around her face,
linger over her shoulders,
and she smiles with teeth shining
like white specs on silky wings,
an image of her in a red bathing suit
permanently pressed
into history's page, never to fade.

In another photo, on the set of Charlie's Angles,
she stares into a tennis racket-sized mirror,
admires her winged locks illuminating her
youth—the golden coins of her worth—
stares like she is looking at her reflection
in a drop of rain on a flower,
wondering, *how long can a butterfly live?*

After O'Neil left her, it is said she flew away
for hours at a time. I can almost see her
circling around her room on a cloud of cannabis
and tequila. Before she transformed
back into caterpillar, she must have
crash-landed on her dresser, fallen
onto her bed, wrapped in a cocoon
of blanket, her winged hair flattened,
her face pressed into pillow.

I Need Dramamine

"My flippers cripple me, I crawl like an insect down the ladder and there is no one to tell me when the ocean will begin."
—Adrienne Rich, "Diving into the Wreck"

Already I see my pre-teen daughter shedding
her shell, inching away from fluid movements,
steady as a stream, tumbling toward tumultuous,
oceanic insecurity.
Already she thinks her blonde friend is more popular,
complains she has "owl eyes," practices
rouging her cheeks. She is a baby lady.
Soon, movie star images and social media will swallow her
in their cavernous mouths, while I watch—
stranded on the shoreline. I want to keep her
busy little hands crafting meaningful art
because already I see them suctioned
like tentacles around her phone—
that stifled, tiny universe. I see
her authentic self slowly molting
as she swims seaward toward confusion
to dive into that wreck.

A Chat with My Daughter about a Woman and Her Vase

Influenced by a viewing of R.C. Gorman's Salina

The way the ground and sky are
painted caramel colors during dusk,
and the way Salina wears white
like vanilla ice cream,
her hair a chocolate fudge spill
dripping down her back, reminds me
of cravings boys will have
when they encounter females
in that space between childhood
and womanhood, shown here as pottery
fresh out of the kiln, newly painted
with groups of claw-like swirls
groping this vase, and Salina
appears as a desert dessert waiting
outside of her bowl. See how,
with chin raised, she proudly protects
her virgin vase? She waits for a love
to warm her skin like the sun's fingers,
waits for her heart to fully flower.

How We Lie under an Olive Tree

Sounds of wing flaps tap tepid air.
Kalamata kisses burst inside my mouth.
Clocks have disappeared with passing night
as my pen presses breath into black words
Long leaves hang like skirt fringe from branches.
Rooftops bleed blue into ocean's sway,
and sky turns gray where sun clung, yesterday.
Each moment looms under cumulus threat:
heavy clouds push my cold shoulders down.
It is possible to feel over-loved, he says,
People are not planted like trees, he adds.
Then, a wise wind snatches my paper away:
       one line short of a sonnet.

Three Odes to a Tactile Past

1.

There is nothing
quite like a breakup call
in a phone booth.
The glass doors close
on the soundproof mime:
a show that begins when
the black handset becomes
a barbell weight
so heavy it must be cradled
with a neck.
The coins clink
like tiny tin doors
slamming on last words,
while fingertips press hard
and hesitant on
each
stubborn
button.
Meanwhile, the mixture
of whiskey and cologne
still alive in the mouthpiece
holes, a gift leftover
by the last stranger,
causes a surprise buzz,
and the steel cold cord coils
snake-like, ready to squeeze.
I didn't know then
the booth would become
an upright coffin
holding the remains

of a lost love: a crying body
with shoulders slumped
like a tree hunched
heavy with storm.

2.

                    The button snaps on,
the machine hums. Ink punctuates air with petroleum:
                    I will drive it to a destination.
The metal keys clack toward progress, each press
                    its own exclamation point.

Steel type-bars lift like spiders walking across the page
                    until the heavy platen thuds
like a boot kicking me on to the next line. Mistakes are
whitewashed
                    with Monet dots
leaving the wet ink that remains to shine triumphant.

3.
                              The album cover
                    is shrink-wrapped art. A shiny vinyl gift
                    of mystery, how the needle fits within grooves
                    to give sound. And then to watch it spin around,
              like an orbit shifts time
        until the needle lifts like an orchestra wand
in a conductor's hand at the show's end.

Paper Doll

Make no mistake, I feel the tearing of my edges
when hands release me from a page.
One deviation from a dotted line
could rip me to dismemberment, to a fate
as crumpled as instant trash. My smile belies
my fear, my desire for some pair of hands
to swaddle my near-naked self with an overlay
of decency. How I have many more wishes than this.
How I wish to shed this one-dimensional world,
flee this flat and partial existence to experience
three full sides. How I want to be more than a template
for fashion, more than a pretty shadow made of trees.
How I disagree with choices hands make who dress me.
When I dream, I am translucent—
eyes penetrate my skin, bones, and organs—
reveal my thoughts unshackled from the page.
If I were rounded out, you would see I have more
than one facial expression. I can cry,
laugh, furrow my brows into complicated caves
large enough for a human being to enter.

Dating Story Trilogy

The Importance of Breathing Air

She went on a blind coffee date with a man she met online. His voice gurgled wet with strain. Every word trickled up through his larynx from the decomposed depths of his chest as if it were his last. Gremlins lived in his lungs. He was Puff the Magic Wolfman with tiny, furry greenish gremlins huffing, puffing, banging, and building a grand gremlin village inside his body. Perhaps the gremlins believe they are captives, POWs digging tunnels to freedom, crawling along his esophagus and tracheal tube toward fresh air. There was that, and he said Vegas was his favorite vacation spot.

Numbers

TMI took her out for coffee. She said it was a pleasure to meet a 48-year-old teen. She liked that he is laid back and lives in a small apartment in a hip college kid section of the city and plays the drums in a band that plays cover tunes. He told her he wanted to finish only 2 years of college, hates to read books, gave up an opportunity to attend a 4-year college at age 27 because he didn't want any more work, is terrible at math, has had 2 pacemakers in the past 4 years, keeps his 80 lb. dog in a crate all day, and so far, 5 women have lost interest in him after 5 dates.

Mechanomorphism

Last night she dated Let You Entertain Me. She could see his invisible remote control aimed at her: click, "tell me something surprising about you." Click, "I want to be challenged at every turn." Click, "What are you wearing?" Click, "Make me laugh." And it turned her off.

Rain After Good-bye

I walk without an umbrella, uncaring
as mist aerosols my face,
skinny cold fingers pick through my hair,
even as it turns to acupuncture,
needles my neck after it transforms—
at the corner of 10th and Madison—
into piercing rain moving skyward
from an angry ground.

At home, I peel off heavy layers, shivering
like a feather-weight champion, cornered
as I watch rain strike the horizon,
leave heavy stripes through air,
and ringlets of possibility puncture holes
across the Hudson River. Rain spills
from gutters onto a plaster mermaid
in my yard, and I swear, a grin forms
at the corners of her mouth.

How to Make Boxed Shells: 8 Easy Steps

Fall in love too young. Feel heat rise to a boil, cleave to him until you turn tender. Say "YES!" half asleep when he slips a ring around your toothbrush. Finish your studies and move around the country to look for yourself as he looks for himself. Let your ideals of marriage drain out through the holes of your skin. Pretend you found yourselves. Mix together and melt like butter into a town
the two of you agree upon—not too city for him—not too country for you. Decide it's a good idea to have a baby *before* you begin an illustrious career with your Bachelor of Arts degree in English. Continue stirring. Leave him when you discover him stuck like powdered cheese to the side of his twenties during his thirties and forties. Work part time, go back to school full time, scrub your dirty pot of a house, ignore disorder in your car and every closet—
perfection clearly beyond your energy level. In your free time, keep your kids alive. Stand half asleep at the stove stirring and stirring until you become one with the macaroni, stick to your obligations like alfredo sauce. Carve creative words out of the empty box you threw away in your chest—that unrelenting space that patiently waits for something more as you chew, and chew, and chew.

Cobra Pose

I writhe on the floor in this ironic position,
proud head tilting back,
thinking men are the belly-dragging kind,
screwing their way through holes
with their reptilian genitals,
sliding through grass
all venom and muscle. Still
this pose exposes me:
I have charmed snakes from their tightly woven baskets.
I have lied and slithered through love,
left long impressive trails of my own ugly dead skin.

3.

Wild Thing

Wild Thing Pose

dear body,

when we were sickened with flu,
every molecule of you screamed at me
from within like it was a coup,
and i could no longer ignore you.
all of those years i inhaled burnt energy sticks
as if killing you slowly a suitable gift,
surging agitation, a feasible replacement for rest.
for four years, i rationed your food,
starved you to bones until your clothes hung like sails,
until i smiled at a scale. and one of the times
i drank us to the floor, we were roofied
for fun. in the morning we awoke naked
with broken nails. you puked for twelve hours.
fists pounded for another twelve on walls
inside your head. you humble me,
it turns out, you know i am capable
of loving bodies, of caring for babies,
and you cried missiles inside of me,
unleashed pains and coughs, chills and sweat,
to get me to flip from wild thing to calm.

At Whole Foods

She is young, maybe 15, tall. Her long limbs
are skin-covered sticks, cheeks still plump
with baby fat. Her eyes dart around
the produce section, suspicious of loose food
as if it would jump from bins, force its way
down her throat into her sunken belly.
I watch as she walks, followed by her mother.
My chubby baby girl gnaws a peach, faces me
in our cart as the skinny girl presses her face
against the lettuce case as if studying relics
in a museum, forbidden to touch. Her mother
keeps her distance, pushes an empty cart, peers
into the glass after her, hoping
to find answers. I remember this part of therapy
from my youth: slow integration, empowerment.
Next, the girl floats among bulk bins with palpable awe,
observes the strange, caged food from her safe place
in the aisle. With controlled hands at her sides,
she thinks food is a predator. If set free, it would attack
her fat cells, puff her up like a hippo.
If she doesn't eat, the doctor will strap her to a bed,
fill her veins with liquid sugar until it turns into fifteen pounds.
Either way, she is a victim. As for me, there will be no models
taped to my daughter's wall, no broken ego to force feed.

Revolved Triangle

Hunched over my desk in a pre-dawn hour,
I eat from my pen like a spoon,
mine my mind for a part of me
I left in a bar after skiing,
I feel opposite of wanting to die:
I feel already dead and wanting to live.
How strange it is that past lovers are strangers
with unfamiliar hands that brushed over my skin,
whose foreign mouths once matched mine.
The obscurity of houses—
how I could travel the same floors for years,
then lose them like trails as if I ran out
of breadcrumbs in the woods. A message
attached to my *Yogi* tea bag says,
I am in the universe, and the universe is in me.
This makes me believe it is possible
to drown inside a teardrop, or grow
roots inside that hold me in place.
Yet even evolution with its steady progression
forward is circular: one day I will bend back to helpless.
Regardless, I will do this pose because
even earth keeps moving her round hips
around and around the sun,
reminding me not to give up.

Postfeminist Halloween Party

How does one dress, postfeminist, as Little Red Riding Hood?
        Should she move confident among the crowd, her blood red
        plastic cup spilling over with brew, unafraid to wear
whatever
        she wants? Does she desire hungry eyes on her skirt,
        fishnet stockings, stilettos, tight red half shirt?
        Is she no longer obedient, eager to please
        her ailing grandma with baskets of baked goods?
Or does she walk past racks at the Halloween shop
        beckoning her to succumb to trends? Does she
        fashion a shawl, button up her form,
        force eyes to face her gaze, instead?
Who is Red Riding Hood at *this* party?
        A wolf, part of the pack, a huntress in the night
        programmed to think she will accept nothing less?
And might this mean she is even more lost in the woods?

Circling Heart Pose

Frowny faced emojis paddle through quiet tears,
     stream down my face in hot yoga.
Others swim lanes through my veins.
     My body blends blood into a genetic cocktail,
mixes with DNA from a grandfather I never met,
     lost at 45 to a pack-a-day *Camel* fatality.
Longevity hovers over my mat
     like a question mark, and sadness
having never heard his voice
     say grandfather words. Light lures my eyes
to a swaying Eastern redbud outside:
     its branches spread wide for a hug,
its stemmed fingers reach out to comfort,
     offers me handfuls of heart-shaped leaves.

Reflection on R.C. Gorman's *Reflection*

She hovers over cold water
colored a blue more alarming than
       a Southwest sky.

The lavender sand, empty
of whiskered cacti could mean
       a lover's drought.

She could topple in
to her wet death,
       like Ophelia.

Or, alone at last, freed from weaving,
 man, children, hearth,
       she searches

her reflection for her smile,
which must have fallen under
       the surface.

Instead, she finds the moon,
a thin sliced frown. The round ripples
       suggest speech,

as if the moon tells her happiness
hides out of sight
       and within.

Mountain Lessons

After *Earth Mother,* R.C. Gorman, serigraph on paper

Earth, dusted with flaky desert skin,
grips this new mother covered with skin like sunsets.
Earth offers her windy voice and cacti warnings
as abrasive as burned crop fields,
an eight-hundred-mile walk to *Bosque Redondo,*
and heartbreak.
The cacti cast shadows that loom,
and under the moon, this new mother whispers,
     don't linger too long in their shadows.
Earth hears her lessons passed on, and her cheeks warm
the air with sun. The new mother is a small hill hunched
in woven yarn sitting on Earth's lap, protected by her
purple mountainous shoulders, and her shawl's fringe
dances in the wind like Earth's thirsty brown grass.

I See This Sculpture and Think My Back is *Not* a Bridge

After R.C. Gorman's *Laughing Sisters,* bronze casting, 1981

Laughing Sisters Study

First, he sketched the sisters sitting upright:
connected lines meld each one into the other,
but then he saw a problem: their backs as walls
could be scaled or climbed with a ladder pressed against them.
Instead, Gorman casts these sisters with convex spines
arching into upside down bridges: un-crossable.

Bronze

Color of coffee stirred with sunshine, clay
carved into bowls, pots, a woman's throbbing heart.
Color of desert plant stems used for baby beds,
the artist's hands as he poured these molten bronze sisters.
Color of strength, more lasting than marble, copper,
a King George III statue melted into freedom's weapon.

1981 Break Out

These sisters laugh because they know
Earth is our mother. We are here because she pushed us
through her canyon walls, nursed us with her honeyed breasts.
She cradles us until our last breath billows out,
until we lie buried inside her loamy womb.
Gorman made sisters holding hands
and laughing because they will outlast us.

Gracias!

After R.C. Gorman's *Gracias*

Her hair and shawl blend in
        with blue/black sky.
Stars match her eyes,
        pink flowers, her skirt
and what hides beneath.
        I bet sky peers down,
sees her as a taller flower
        waiting for pollen.
Maybe she bargains
        with the Great Spirit,
avoids stamen spray,
        saves her seeds for a time
when men work through
        their confusion
between love and lust
        as if their two hands
can't hold onto both.
        And when love slips
through their fists,
        earth heats up, lust
lures them to her
        comely chamber full
of flooding glaciers,
        and she floats naked
among fallen forests.
        Gracias for passing
over my petals,
        this woman whispers
every month as she
        stares inside sky's
hungry open mouth.

Money as Factory

—For all of the women politicians out there

Honey, in this town diluted cotton and linen pulp pours
        into a mold to be smoothed into wet sheets and dried.
Presidential portraits roll off the press in a blur,
        and I use them to buy proper pearls for my ears and throat,
a suit hemmed below my knees, use the green
        for my short, tidy hair, a statement of feminine-
masculine initiative that gets the job done. Politics,
        after all, is where it's at, is where I'm heading:
to the pulpit for a broadcast on women's rights
        in surround sound, while the media asks me,
"Who takes care of your son when you're
        off campaigning?"
And they may call me aggressive, fierce, hard,
        "ball-busting and overemotional."
And they will comment on my appearance, regardless
        of the iron-clad care I exert for that display,
even though across town I see business owners
        pin dollars on walls behind registers for luck,
pin up my sisters on walls in back rooms
        as if they could leap down and dance
        some shimmy, so well hidden behind dignity's surface,
        and fellow senators in this town will shove fistfuls of bills
down bras—the lips of presidents
        smashed against their skin
        to imprint value on them.

Chair Pose

Bend your knees, press
feet together, sit back.

Reach your hands skyward
past glass ceilings.

Depend upon nothing
but your strength.

Let your legs and arms be
balanced, hold you planted

into earth: indestructible
Sequoia, solid and rooted.

Do not expect
anything to appear.

There is only you
& a chair of air.

Prepare to learn
to sit without.

Life Broken into Thirds

After R.C. Gorman's Proud Lady

Outside, cicadas schemed in trees,
smoldered wood fell to ash,
and smoke rose into a moonless night.

She kicked frigid sticks off of her path,
frightened to enter her empty nest,
touched her way to a lonely chair,

and crossed her legs into a heart.
Her fingers fastened beads around her neck, and then
she washed her feelings back to white.

Mountain Pose

I am a mountain of woman a mountain of mountains
men want to climb a mountain of beginnings and endings
a mountain to ski down to climb on to speak to slide down
I am a mountain of resistance I am a mountain of mountain
lions and mountain liars a mountain a mutton would be proud
of purple and mountainous spacious and elevated a mountain
with fountains to run through I am a mountain who wonders
what a mountain must do to get a mountain around here.

Goddess Pose

I feel like a goddess must feel,
like a tropical rainforest bursting
rivers lined with hovering trees,
heavy with green. My problems fall
down waterfalls, vaporize into steam
painted by rainbows wrapped around
the gift of sky. I begin to find
the beginning of my twisting vines.
My body feels wet with air, sweats,
drowns from sounds—shrieks and hums,
the drum of rain. I realize the sky
sees me less a mountain full of lava,
more a seismic quake who shakes
and splits open to birth Mojave,
sees me hug my feet to the ground,
so I don't fall off, become lost, tossed into space.

Sisterhood

I notice sun has bedazzled this water.
Shiny gems fastened to this wide rolling cloth topple,
sparkle and blend together into waves.
Pelicans ignore the adornment,
dive below its glitter for sustenance.

A ship carries important items over this gleam,
and I watch how the ocean delivers radiance,
tosses the vessel, churns shimmer to white foam.

What if I found peace in the sea's shuffling,
let the pressure to measure my glimmer fall away?
What if I let myself flow into luminous energy
and radiate off neighboring waves?

      Could women behave like an ocean?
      Could we turn lustrous under sun,
      become a collective brilliance,
      move forward over crest and trough
      together—
adrift a fourth wave—
      swell with the strength it will take
      to change a shoreline?

If This Chair Could Talk

After photograph by R.C. Gorman, 1980

"This is Aunt Mary's chair, which doesn't look like a throne, but it is.
    She's a queen."

—*R.C. Gorman*

At the epicenter of settled dust, her chair
sits fading and cracking under sunray
pressure like a field laborer's sad face.
If it could talk, we would hear stories
spanning thirty years or more about her
holding lap after lapful of babies, shucked corn, potatoes.
It would mention what is not in black and white,
beyond the chicken resting in its shade,
footprints in dirt, chipped window paint.
It would tell us the chair's busted-out
seams trap Aunt Mary's laugh,
and they (a chicken and a chair) wait patiently
for her return. "I'm worn out," the chair might say,
but sunlight hits one of its stainless-steel legs
and begs to differ, makes it glisten
like a 7 lb., 6 oz. Imperial Crown.

New Love

It appears I fell in. No, I dove into this
in reverse birth. I recognize this smeared feeling,
submerged again in a salty womb, untethered
to another chance. With eyes closed,
face blurred, I must look like a sonogram photo
frozen in place among waves for a moment.
Bubbles around my face carry air from my lungs:
a possibility for suffocation   or freedom.
Gone is the tedious half-strained lip quiver
left after lies from my past life, from a love
lost. How many seconds before I come out
cleanly licked by seaweed tongues?
How long before old fingerprints float
off of my skin, swallowed by fish?
When my eyes open at last, will I see
colors and details on a face? Will I
recognize my new love's voice?

Lotus Pose

If I am a flower
who blooms and dies,
I am a lotus
who rises from sinking sand.
Sun awakens me
only to push me through
a sticky wet womb
into light, until my petals
unfold and float incandescent
above each day's failed attempt
to drown me in its mud.

About the Author

Brenda Nicholas is the author of the chapbook, *Hari Om, Hurry Home* (Finishing Line Press, 2021). Her work has appeared or is forthcoming in *Sand Hills Literary Magazine, Evening Street Review, Unbroken, The Painted Bride Quarterly, The Ekphrastic Review,* among others. Nicholas completed her MFA in Creative Writing at UNCW in 2016 and is an Associate Professor of English at Temple College in Texas.

Kelsay Books
Kelsaybooks.com

www.ingramcontent.com/pod-product-compliance
Lightning Source LLC
Chambersburg PA
CBHW071355090426
42738CB00012B/3133